Pebble® Plus

Investigate the Seasons

Let's Look at Summer

Revised Edition

by Sarah L. Schuette

T0044784

CAPSTONE PRESS
a capstone imprint

Pebble Plus is published by Capstone Press,
1710 Roe Crest Drive, North Mankato, Minnesota 56003
www.mycapstone.com

**Library of Congress Cataloging-in-Publication Data
is available on the Library of Congress website.**

ISBN 978-1-5435-0859-8 (library binding)
ISBN 978-1-5435-0875-8 (paperback)
ISBN 978-1-5435-0879-6 (ebook pdf)

Editorial Credits
Sarah Bennett, designer; Tracy Cummins, media researcher,
Laura Manthe, production specialist

Photo Credits
Alamy: F. Rauschenbach, 11; Shutterstock: Artens, 21,
ConstantinosZ, Cover, Fer Gregory, 13, Garsya, 3, LazarenkoD,
7, Liubou Yasiukovich, Cover Design Element, majeczka, 5,
martin33, 17, Marty Nelson, 9, Sergey Kotelnikov, 19, vblinov, 15,
WDG Photo, 1

Note to Parents and Teachers

The Investigate the Seasons set supports national science
standards related to weather and life science. This book
describes and illustrates the season of summer. The images
support early readers in understanding the text. The repetition
of words and phrases helps early readers learn new words. This
book also introduces early readers to subject-specific vocabulary
words, which are defined in the Glossary section. Early readers
may need assistance to read some words and to use the Table of
Contents, Glossary, Read More, Internet Sites, Critical Thinking
Questions, and Index sections of the book.

Table of Contents

It's Summer!

How do you know

it's summer?

The temperature rises.

It's the warmest season.

The sun shines high
in the sky.
Summer days are
the longest of the year.

Animals in Summer

What do animals do

in summer?

Deer rest in the shade

to keep cool.

Tadpoles grow

into young frogs.

They find lots of bugs to eat.

Fireflies light up

on summer nights.

They flash to find mates.

Plants in Summer

What happens to plants

in summer?

Trees are full

of green leaves.

Plump cherries hang
from branches.
They are a tasty
summer treat.

Sunflowers turn

toward the sun.

They grow taller

with the warm sunshine.

What's Next?

The weather gets colder.

Summer is over.

What season comes next?

Glossary

mate—a partner or one of a pair; fireflies flash their lights to attract mates

season—one of the four parts of the year; winter, spring, summer, and fall are seasons

shade—an area out of the sun

tadpole—a young frog; tadpoles hatch from eggs and swim in water

temperature—the measure of how hot or cold something is

Read More

Owen, Ruth. *How Do You Know It's Summer?* Signs of the Seasons. New York: Bearport Publishing, 2017.

Pettiford, Rebecca. *Summer.* Seasons of the Year. Minneapolis: Bellwether Media, 2018.

Rice, William B. *The Seasons.* Earth and Space Science. Huntington Beach, Calif.: Teacher Created Materials, 2015.

Internet Sites

Use FactHound to find Internet sites related to this book.

Visit *www.facthound.com*

Just type **9781543508598** and go.

Check out projects, games and lots more at
www.capstonekids.com

Critical Thinking Questions

1. What happens to the days during summer?

2. How do deer stay cool in summer?

3. Describe how you stay cool during the season of summer.

Index